LEARN
TOGETHER

PUNCTUATION
PRACTICE

Capital letters, commas, full stops; jokes and poems to read aloud

Sandra Soper

A Piccolo Original
Piccolo Books

Notes for parents

Punctuation is about making sense of what we write. It is not about rules and regulations which are fixed once and forever. Last century's punctuation is not ours and ours will not be the same a hundred years from now.

Language came before punctuation and the latter should always serve the former – never the other way round. Punctuation exercises therefore should not get in the way of a child's enjoyment of language.

Spelling activities are included throughout this book because spelling, too, is about making sense of what we write so that others can understand what we mean.

The activities in this book bring the child into contact with poetry and prose which is enjoyable in itself. This should help the child to see the punctuation exercises as worth doing and enjoyable.

Generally speaking, too much emphasis on the mechanics of punctuation hinders rather than helps a child's writing. A light handed approach and consistent regular practice will help a child's skill in punctuation to develop almost automatically. With all this in mind, the work in this book is intended to be enjoyed. The more a child enjoys it, the more she will want to do and the more she does, the better she will become.

Capitals, Full Stops, Nouns

Read the poem aloud, underline the capitals and circle the full stops.

The Common Cormorant

The common <u>cormorant</u> or <u>shag</u>
lays <u>eggs</u> inside a paper <u>bag</u>.
The <u>reason</u> you will see no <u>doubt</u>
is to keep the <u>lightning</u> out.
But what these unobservant <u>birds</u>
have never noticed is that <u>herds</u>
of wandering <u>bears</u> may come with <u>buns</u>
and steal the bags to hold the <u>crumbs</u>.

The underlined words are nouns (or names of things). Write the nouns out in alphabetical order. Look up the meanings in a dictionary and write them out.

_____ _____

_____ _____

_____ _____

_____ _____

_____ _____

_____ _____

_____ _____

_____ _____

_____ _____

_____ _____

Spelling – silent gh

Wrong spellings can muddle the meaning of what you are trying to write. Correct spellings, like punctuation, help the reader understand. Read the words aloud. Cover them, then write each word again. Check the spelling.

caught _____   brought _____
taught _____   fought _____
haughty _____   nought _____
naughty _____   brought _____
daughter _____   thought _____

Find the ten words above in the box below.

a	e	n	o	u	g	h	t	b	f	c	h	d	b	t
f	c	a	u	g	h	t	a	y	o	d	a	h	r	h
b	o	u	g	h	t	l	u	o	u	m	u	l	o	o
n	p	g	q	r	s	t	g	u	g	d	g	w	u	u
y	z	h	a	w	t	h	h	s	h	o	h	e	g	g
m	o	t	s	l	b	c	t	w	t	g	t	l	h	h
b	f	y	d	a	u	g	h	t	e	r	y	m	t	t

Copy the verse.

Advice to the Candidate
Gain a thoroughly
good result
through thorough
thoughtful practice.

4

Commas

Read the verses aloud then circle the commas.

Mary had a little lamb,
a lobster and some prunes,
a glass of milk, a piece of pie,
and then some macaroons.

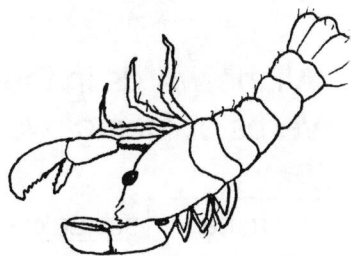

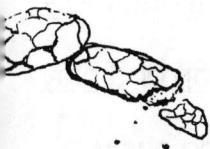

It made the busy waiters grin
to see her order so,
and when they carried Mary out,
her face was white as snow.

Write out the verses again and go over the commas in red. Draw a picture to illustrate your verses.

_____

_____

_____

_____

_____

_____

_____

_____

Nouns and Verbs

All the words in the boxes are nouns. The words underlined are verbs or 'doing' words.

mice	squeak		horns	toot		farmers	plant and sow
people	speak		owls	hoot		mowers	cut and mow
birds	fly		piglets	squeal		kittens	leap and play
babies	cry		bells	peal		bad	dreams	go away

Nouns	Verbs
owls	hoot
turkeys	gobble
cocks	crow
birds	fly
bakers	bake
mowers	mow
knitters	knit
strikers	shoot
drivers	drive
robbers	take
farmers	sow
sitters	sit
divers	dive
children	squabble
babies	cry
crops	grow
stars	shine

Choose words from the table and add more of your own to make up some rhyming verses.

_____

_____

_____

_____

_____

_____

_____

_____

_____

_____

Capitals and Full Stops

Written sentences begin with a capital letter and end with a full stop. The names of places also start with a capital letter. Read the sentences below, then underline the capital letters and circle the full stops.

The highest mountains in the world are the Himalayas. The highest mountain in the range is Mount Everest.

The Himalayas stretch in a downward curve right across the top of India, separating it from Tibet to the north.

The Rocky Mountains are the highest mountains in Canada. They are on the west coast and continue south into the United States.

The Alps are the highest mountains in Europe. They appear in several countries, including Switzerland, Southern France and Northern Italy.

Answer these questions in a sentence.

In which mountain range is Mount Everest?

_____

Which country is north of India?

_____

Which country is south of Canada?

_____

Which range of mountains appears in several Central European countries?

_____

Apostrophes

Sometimes when we speak, we run words together leaving out one or two letters. When the words are written down, an apostrophe ☐ shows there are missing letters.

I can no̲t ——► I can't   I do n o̲ t ——► I don't

I ha̲d ——► I'd   You ha̲ve ——► You've

Rewrite the sentences. Leave out the apostrophes and write in the missing letters.

Joe didn't mean to break the ruler, but he wasn't exactly using it sensiby either.

_____

_____

"Joe! You've gone too far this time m'lad," cried Ms Black.

_____

_____

She pointed to the seat by the door. "There's your seat till Friday."

_____

_____

"We've wasted enough time now. It's half past nine already."

_____

_____

I'd better finish this or she'll write to my dad again, thought Joe.

_____

_____

Ms Black looked at her watch. "They'll do this for ten minutes, then we'll have a quiz before assembly."

_____

_____

Spelling – ph saying 'f'

Copy the word and draw a box round the ph sound. Cover, then write the word again from memory. Check the spelling.

elephant
elephant
elephant

nephew

paragraph

alphabet

telephone

triumph

sphere

physician

photograph

geography

pheasant

pharmacy

Down
Large grey mammal

Down
We have 26 letters in ours

Across
Image recorded by a camera

Across
My sister's son

Across
A solid circle

Down
Device for transmitting speech

Across
Medicines are prepared and dispensed here

Down
Another word for doctor

Down
The study of places and people

Across
A victory or major achievement

Punctuation Matters

Read the verse aloud, pausing at the end of each line. Draw a picture to go with it.

> Caesar entered on his head
>
> A helmet on each foot
>
> A sandal in his hand he had
>
> His trusty sword to boot

Rewrite the verse and punctuate it like this:

put a comma after **entered**, **helmet** and **sandal**, and a full stop after **boot**. Draw the picture to go with this verse.

_____

_____

_____

_____

Find out from a dictionary what 'to boot' means and write the meaning here.

_____

Read the notices aloud.

PRIVATE

NO SWIMMING

ALLOWED

is not the same as

PRIVATE ?

NO.

Swimming Allowed

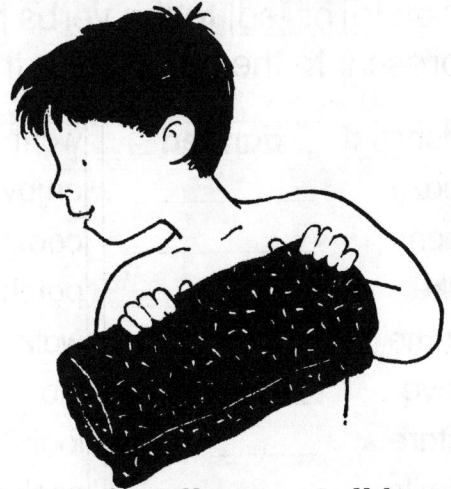

Choose another group of words – for example, **silence**, **talking,
no**, **allowed**.
Use line length, a full stop and a question mark in different ways to
change the meaning of the group of words. Illustrate the notice.

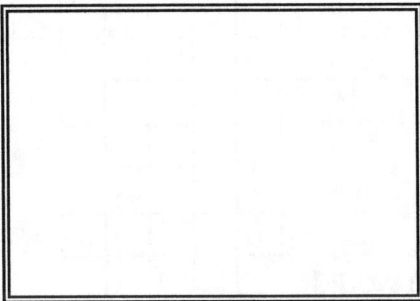

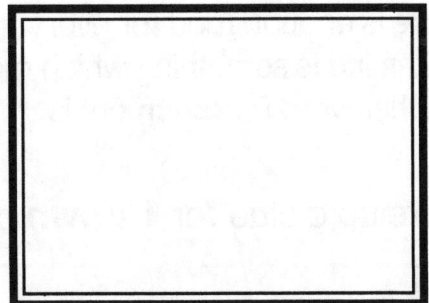

Present and Past Tense

Use the correct tense to help make your writing clearer. This sentence is wrong.

> I play on the swing last night.

Write the correct version here.

Add ⬚d or ⬚ed to the verbs below to change them from the present to the past tense, then write the whole word

dance **d** __danced__	want _____	scare _____
gaze _____	enjoy _____	scratch _____
ache _____	cook _____	cycle _____
like _____	patch _____	munch _____
tame _____	walk _____	wash _____
love _____	play _____	jump _____
stare _____	look _____	crash _____
smile _____	pack _____	live _____
share _____	chew _____	laugh _____
debate _____	talk _____	care _____

Fill the boxes with the past or present tense of a verb.

The prisoner bent the bars back and ....

When I bumped my head it ....

Before I learnt to walk I had to ....

I go on holiday tomorrow, so tonight I must ....

Don't gawp at me like that. It's rude to ....

The first time I fell off my bike I really had a ....

There is enough food for everyone if only we would ....

Swimming is something which most children ....

Another word for argument is ....

Make up a clue for **I down** and write it here.

_____

Commas

Read the poem aloud, pausing at the commas. Circle all the commas.

The Carnivorous Cow

A dairyman, living near Slough,
was missing, and no one knew how
till his foreman was able
to look in the stable,
where they kept a remarkable cow.

This creature had plenty of roots,
and a good share of young turnip shoots.
What seems rather strange,
is it longed for a change,
so ate a man, down to his boots.

Commas can affect the meaning of words.

> A dairyman living,
> near Slough was missing.

> A dairyman,
> living near Slough,
> was missing.

In the first sentence we are told where the dairyman was missing. In the second we are told where he lived, but not where he was missing.

Rewrite the sentences and omit the commas to change the meaning.

The coat, rack and umbrella stand were missing.
The coat rack and umbrella stand were missing.

The door, knob and light switch were tested for fingerprints.

Ink had stained Jo's finger, nail and cuticle blue.

During February snow covered the garage, roof and shed.

Phil's football, boots and laces were caked with thick mud.

Harry's car, door and bumper were badly dented in the crash.

Adjectives – Comparative and Superlative

An adjective is used to describe something – **big** lorry.
When we are comparing two things we use a <u>Comparative</u>
<u>Adjective</u> – **bigger** lorry. When we are comparing more than two
things we use a <u>Superlative</u> <u>Adjective</u> – **biggest** lorry.

Use the pattern to complete the table.

fast ———————▶	faster ———————▶	fastest
slow		
young		
old		
bright		
dull		
great		
little		
early		
late		

Two exceptions to the pattern are **good/ better/ best**,
some/ more/ most.

Copy these to practise your handwriting.

<u>Endeavour</u>

Good better best
Never let it rest
Till the good is better
And the better best

<u>Generosity</u>

Some more most
Do not count the cost
Give some then some more
To those who need it most

Spelling – ch saying 'k'

Read, then copy the word. Draw a box round the ch sound. Cover, then write the word again from memory. Check the spellings.

school	chord	scheme	Christ
school			
school			

echo	stomach	chemist	Christmas

mechanic	orchestra	character	Christian

Across

1 Where Mary's lamb followed her one day
4 A group of musical notes sounded together
5 A person who looks after machinery
7 Organ of the body which digests food

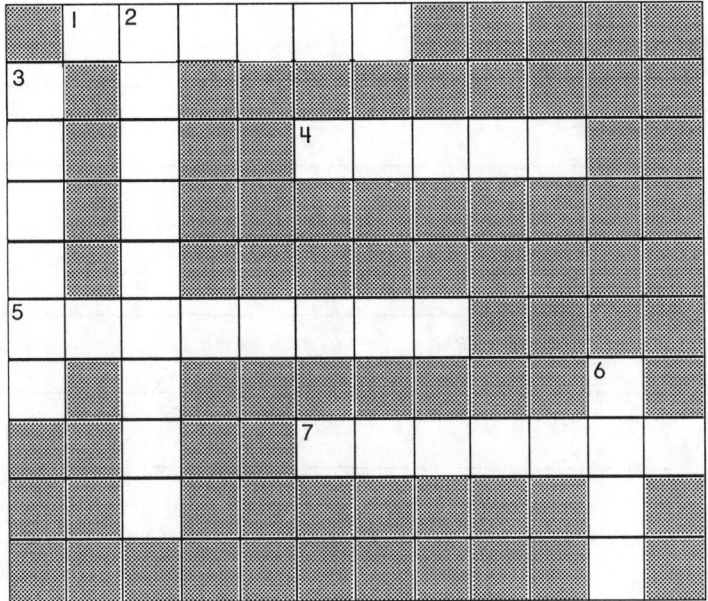

Down

2 A person represented in a play
3 A plan
6 A sound that is heard again after it bounces back off something solid.

Adjectives

Read the poem aloud.

The Bells of Heaven

'Twould ring the bells of Heaven
The <u>wildest</u> peal for years,
If Parson lost his senses
And people came to theirs,
And he and they together
Knelt down with <u>angry</u> prayers
For <u>tamed</u> and <u>shabby</u> tigers
And <u>dancing</u> dogs and bears,
And <u>wretched</u>, <u>blind</u> pit ponies,
And <u>little</u> <u>hunted</u> hares.

Ralph Hodgson

The underlined words are adjectives – words that tell you what someone or something is like. Write the underlined words in alphabetical order below. Use a dictionary to look up the meanings, then write them out.

_____   _____

_____   _____

_____   _____

_____   _____

_____   _____

_____   _____

_____   _____

Opposites

Rewrite the words, adding the prefix shown at the top of each column to change the word to its opposite.

dis		un		in	
advantage		comfortable		correct	
approve		common		convenient	
connect		fair		human	
content		just		sane	
loyal		kind		visible	
order		necessary		audible	

Read the passage, then underline any words from above that you can find.

"You're insane Pip," I said when I found him under my bed. His mop of red hair was just visible by the corner.
"I'm not insane, I'm only human like you."
"Well, I don't keep running away, do I?"
I s'pose he was at a disadvantage. He thought his new dad didn't approve of him.
"He seems fair enough to me," I said.
"Yeah, he's fair enough I s'pose, but I still feel it's inconvenient to have me around. He's not content to let me be. It's 'Pip get that hair cut', 'Pip get this room in order', 'Pip that is not correct'. I don't feel comfortable at home anymore."
"I'll have to tell dad you're here."
"Aw, is that really necessary?"
"Pip, you know it is." Feeling a bit uncomfortable and disloyal, I went off to find my dad.

Question Marks and Speech Marks

Read the jokes and circle the question marks and speech marks.

What did the robot say to the petrol pump?

"Take your finger out of your ears when I'm talking to you."

What did the policeman say to his tummy?

"You're under a vest."

Join the right answer to each question. Write out the whole thing again and put in the necessary speech marks.

Doctor doctor I feel like an apple.

You need a book on raising children.

Doctor doctor my child has just fallen down a well.

Well come in then, I won't bite you.

Question Marks and Full Stops

Read the joke. Circle the question mark and full stop.

What's a sleeping bull called?
A bulldozer.

Write the correct answer under each question. Put in the question mark and full stop.

What do you call a boomerang that won't come back

Why did the orange go to the doctor

Where do cows go on holiday

How do you make an apple puff

What do you get if you lie down under a cow

How do you cut the sea in half

What do you give a hurt lemon

Chase it round the garden

Because it wasn't peeling well

Lemonade

Moo York

A pat on the head

A stick

With a sea-saw

Verbs and Adverbs

An adverb adds to the meaning of the verb by telling you how, when or where something happens, for example, **scream piercingly.** Choose suitable adverbs to go with each verb. Write the complete phrase in the middle column.

VERBS		ADVERBS
walk	_____	well
hum	_____	slowly
sing	_____	soundly
sleep	_____	warmly
breathe	_____	sweetly
shout	_____	heartily
eat	_____	loudly
speak	_____	outside
smile	_____	clearly
play	_____	warmly
bleed	_____	brightly
shine	_____	profusely

Answer each clue with one of the phrases above.

You have to do this on a bad telephone line.   _____ _____

You will probably do this after a hard day's work. _____ _____

You will do this in order to be heard.   _____ _____

The full moon does this.   _____ _____

You will do this when you are hungry.   _____ _____

You will do this if you are cut.   _____ _____

Adverbs in Poems

Adverbs can help to paint a clearer picture. Underline the adverbs in the following poems.

Cat crouches silently;
waiting.
Bird pecks hungrily;
unaware
of the lurking danger.

Child sleeps soundly;
dreaming.
Mother smiles lovingly;
hopeful
for the coming years.

Old man walks slowly;
pondering.
Wife looks on fondly;
thinking
over past memories.

Write your own poem. Draw a picture to illustrate it.

Spelling – Words ending in le

Read, then copy the word. Draw a box around the last two letters. Cover then write the word again from memory. Check the spelling.

beetle   scribble   candle   cradle
beetle
beetle

toggle   stable   poodle   jungle

eagle   riddle   treacle   thimble

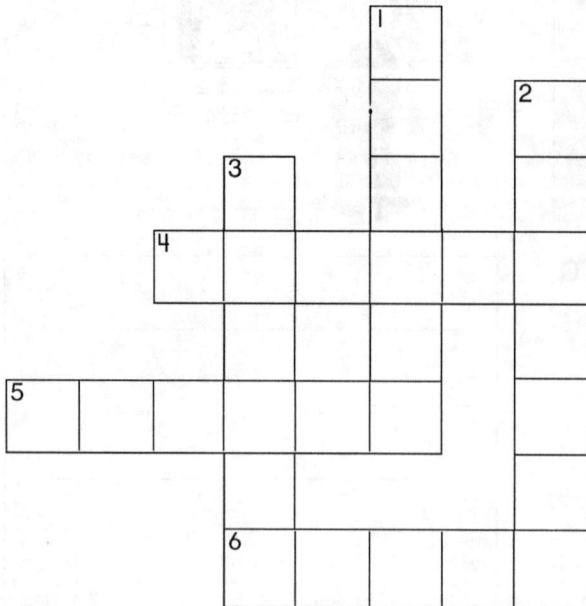

Across
4   A fastening
5   A kind of word puzzle
6   A large bird

Down
1   Dense tropical forest
2   A spire on a church
3   A breed of dog

Letter Writing

Fill in your name in the letter below. Read the letter then write a reply.

15 Court Road
Mayton
SE12 1ST

16.4.92

Dear

Thanks for your letter. Your bike sounds great. I've never seen lime green wheels. Mine has a puncture at the moment. I hate fixing punctures. Do you ride to school? We're not allowed. What kind of music do you like? Do you have a cassette player? Please send a picture in your next letter and WRITE SOON.

Your pen-pal,   Jo

Exclamation Marks

Generally, these are used too much and in the wrong way. Here are some examples of correct usage. Copy the verses out to practise your handwriting.

PLAIN JANE
'Pudding and pie,'
said Jane – 'Oh my!'
'Which would you rather?'
asked her father.
'Both!' said Jane,
quite bold and plain.

BIRD-SCARING RHYME
'Shoo! all you birds.
Shoo! all you birds.
I'll clap my clapper
and knock you down backwards
Shoo! all you birds.
Shoo!'

'Where are you going, big pig, big pig?'
'I'm going to dig in the garden.'
'In the garden to dig? Disgraceful pig!'
'Beg pardon ma'am, beg pardon.'

Homophones

These words sound similar but have different meanings. Rewrite them in alphabetical order and then write out the meanings, using a dictionary where necessary.

new	aisle	ant	knight	foul	board
knew	isle	aunt	night	fowl	bored

Use the correct words from above to answer the clues below.

a female relative ⟶ [ ]

fed up ↓ [ ]

[ ] ⟵ another word for island

opposite of day ⟶ [ ]

[ ] ⟵ a tiny insect

passage between rows of seats ⟶ [ ]

[ ]
↑
play chess on this

opposite of old ⟶ [ ]

Word Search – Adjectives and Nouns

Find the word in the square then cross it off.

Adjectives

hairy

slimy

furry

greasy

burnt

fried

golden

bald

blue

grand

old

simple

contrary

wooden

baby

e	c	x	v	g	j	h	y	o	p	f	g	h	d	a	r	h	h	k	a	s	d
g	o	h	a	i	r	y	w	l	o	d	j	e	r	p	f	u	r	r	y	w	w
w	s	l	i	m	y	s	n	a	i	l	a	c	l	q	r	w	z	b	x	s	k
w	d	j	a	e	z	p	w	x	g	o	t	e	v	k	i	m	f	w	q	v	t
v	p	q	n	h	p	i	M	n	j	s	w	a	n	o	e	g	g	a	i	f	a
r	t	w	j	l	b	d	a	w	j	a	k	o	f	s	d	w	l	q	o	c	u
n	t	w	e	z	p	e	r	l	e	n	f	w	a	c	l	s	w	a	j	i	n
c	o	n	t	r	a	r	y	o	e	b	r	g	s	h	i	h	a	i	r	w	u
c	k	d	s	o	f	p	a	m	v	u	i	r	e	l	a	e	y	e	s	w	p
w	S	i	m	o	n	d	a	l	g	r	e	a	s	y	w	a	o	f	s	v	l
z	l	s	k	u	b	n	i	q	o	n	d	n	l	e	t	d	w	e	q	o	r
h	s	w	a	l	v	s	b	o	l	t	t	d	o	e	p	a	j	b	m	n	c
s	w	a	b	i	l	b	a	l	d	w	w	o	o	d	e	n	o	c	s	y	e
a	o	c	k	l	f	l	b	d	e	w	s	a	o	e	i	q	c	h	a	i	r
l	u	h	w	k	a	u	y	o	n	d	e	x	i	d	h	k	p	b	s	q	o
r	s	i	m	p	l	e	o	a	c	u	s	n	q	s	p	i	d	e	r	w	a
x	b	p	h	k	c	l	d	x	p	k	e	b	l	a	b	t	u	a	l	s	t
w	i	s	o	d	h	m	o	t	h	e	r	e	p	a	l	t	k	r	w	a	b
t	n	x	k	r	o	w	a	h	e	i	l	a	f	u	v	e	e	o	s	a	p
r	h	k	b	r	t	i	w	z	a	p	t	w	h	e	z	n	p	e	a	r	w

Nouns

swan

spider

snail

kitten

chips

egg

hair

head

eyes

mother

duke

Simon

Mary

chair

bear

Which character from a fairy story or nursery rhyme –

Was frightened by a spider? _____

Had golden hair and ate a bowl of porridge? _____

Had a bald head and fell off a wall? _____

Marched ten thousand men up and down a hill? _____

Went to fetch a dog a bone? _____

Met a man selling pies? _____

Had cockle shells in her garden? _____

Discovered his wooden chair broken? _____

Commas and Classification

Read the verse aloud, then circle all the punctuation marks. Write out a list of your main meals for the past seven days. Put a comma between each meal. Make a verse of it if you can, or copy out this one.

Food Diary
On Sunday we ate lasagne,
on Monday we ate hash,
on Tuesday it was spaghetti,
on Wednesday bangers and mash.
On Thursday was it fish fingers?
On Friday toad in the hole,
Saturday, a lot to do, so
it was only cheese in a roll.

LIST OF MEALS

FOOD DIARY

Sort these foods into sweet and savoury.

Crisps, apples, cheese, custard, bacon, chocolate, pizza, lasagne, banana, marmite, marmalade; beans, jam, jelly.

SWEET	SAVOURY

Spelling – Words ending in sion or tion

Read, then copy the word. Draw a box around the t or s. Cover, then write the word again from memory. Check the spelling.

nation	confusion	explanation	devotion
na[t]ion			
nation			

division	invitation	attention	connection

execution	emotion	television	revision

Use the correct word from above to answer the clues.

Down
Another word for disorder

Across
Another word for sight

Down
A card asking you to a party

Across
A collection of people organised into a single state

Down
Strong feeling

Across
Children watch too much much of this

Letter Writing

Fill in your name, then read the letter. Write a reply below.

> 15 Court Road
> Mayton
> SE12 1ST
>
> 24.4.92
>
> Dear
>
> Thanks for your letter. I liked your photos. Your baby brother looks cute. What's a cycling proficiency test? My pocket money is £1.50p a week. How much do you get? I'm saving up for a new set of wheels for my skate board. Do you have a skate board? I raked about a million leaves on Saturday, but got only 50p extra. My mum can be very stingy at times.
>
> Write soon.   Love,   Jo

Verb Word Search

Read the story through, then underline the verbs.

Once upon a time there was a king who made a proclamation to all his people. It went something like this:
"Whoever can tell the biggest lie will receive an apple of pure gold."
All kinds of people came to have a try. Each time the king shook his head and said, "Mmm, that's all very well, but it could be true." Things went on like this for some time until one day a young lad arrived with a barrel under his arm. His name was Jan. He bowed low to the king.
"Your majesty, I have come for the gold sovereigns you borrowed from me last week."
The king looked astonished. "I never borrowed a single sovereign from you. That's a lie."
"Very well, if it's a lie then give me the golden apple."
The king scratched his head. "Wait a moment, you're right. I've just remembered."
"All the better my liege, then I'll take the barrel of gold sovereigns."
The king realised he had been outwitted, and that was how Jan gained the golden apple.

Find ten of the verbs from the story in the box below.

b	e	a	r	s	a	g	u	q	n	p	l	w	z	a	q	k	o	t	s	d	v	b
u	e	i	c	v	b	n	o	z	c	o	m	e	x	c	i	e	u	d	f	h	j	k
r	x	q	v	c	r	b	w	e	f	g	l	n	z	p	i	r	t	e	l	l	v	n
b	e	x	h	r	w	o	r	e	f	g	v	t	b	a	v	d	w	q	l	y	r	o
c	v	a	e	r	i	w	x	u	q	p	t	n	o	i	m	z	i	b	m	c	x	j
r	a	s	l	j	k	e	c	v	i	t	p	o	r	z	s	d	t	t	a	k	e	b
e	r	y	a	i	u	d	w	m	o	g	e	r	r	v	c	q	t	e	d	i	i	w
x	r	u	w	n	s	a	s	d	a	i	a	b	o	x	y	u	e	p	e	d	f	l
u	i	d	f	g	l	e	c	j	o	v	p	q	w	x	t	e	d	k	k	r	s	h
o	v	g	a	i	n	e	d	i	t	e	a	b	e	v	r	w	t	y	i	r	q	l
g	a	v	k	s	b	e	v	o	r	o	n	l	d	b	a	r	h	a	v	e	c	k

Miscellaneous Marks

Read the proverb, underline the capital letter and circle the punctuation marks. Write a short explanation of the proverb underneath.

A poor worker always blames the tools.

_____

_____

Don't count your chickens before they're hatched.

_____

_____

Every cloud has a silver lining.

_____

_____

All's well that ends well.

_____

_____

One person's meat is another's poison.

_____

_____

Too many cooks spoil the broth.

_____

_____

There are three sets of speech marks in the first verse and two in the second. Read the verses through, then write the speech marks in the correct places.

Shutting the Shutter
A woman to her son did utter
Go, my son, and shut the shutter.
The shutter's shut, the boy did mutter
I cannot shut it any shutter.

Washing Instructions
Wash your face and hands my boy
his Uncle Will insists
But mind you watch your wrist watch
When you wash and rinse your wrists

Read the poem aloud, then circle all the punctuation marks (commas, full stops, colon, semi-colon).

Methuselah

Methuselah ate what he found on his plate,
and never, as people do now,
did he note the amount of the calory count:
he ate it because it was chow.
He wasn't disturbed as at dinner he sat,
devouring a roast or a pie,
to think it was lacking in granular fat
or a couple of vitamins shy.
He cheerfully chewed each species of food,
unmindful of troubles or fears
lest his health might be hurt
by some fancy desert;
and he lived over nine hundred years.

Copy out the first four lines in your best handwriting.